MIND JUKEBOX

A MENTAL PLAYLIST FOR INCLUSIVE LEADERS

DR. CHRISTINE HERRING

PITTSBURGH

Published by Herring Seminars & Consulting, LLC
Pittsburgh, PA, USA
Visit our website at herringseminars.com.

ISBN: 978-1-7362131-1-7
Printed by Oddi in Slovenia
Manufacturing date: 05/2024

First Edition
10 9 8 7 6 5 4 3 2 1

Design and Art Direction: Red Herring Design
Cover and Interior Illustrations: Emily Marko
Cover Photo: Emmai Alaquiva
Turntable, Record, Sky Photos: Shutterstock.com

INTRO

In today's ever-evolving, multifaceted work landscape, the significance of inclusive leadership continues to increase rapidly. This leadership approach cherishes and honors each individual, irrespective of their race, gender, ethnicity, faith, or sexual orientation. Inclusive leadership transcends mere tolerance and acceptance by actively pursuing and nurturing diverse viewpoints, experiences, and abilities. This results in enhanced decision-making, innovation, and growth.

But where does the journey toward inclusive leadership commence? It begins with our mental soundtracks.

You may wonder, what constitutes a mental soundtrack? It's an assortment of attitudes, beliefs, and preconceptions we subconsciously carry with us on a daily basis. These mental soundtracks substantially influence our interactions with the world around us, encompassing our colleagues, communities, and families. As leaders, scrutinizing our mental soundtracks and consciously "remixing" them is crucial in becoming more inclusive.

In this exploration of inclusive leadership, we introduce two guiding concepts: "footprints" and "handprints."

Footprints, in this context, are the unintentional or even intentional acts that cause harm, often leaving indelible marks on the people and environments we encounter. These may be the biases we unconsciously hold, the stereotypes we unwittingly perpetuate, or the exclusions we unintentionally commit. Recognizing our footprints is essential, for awareness is the first step in changing our harmful patterns.

Conversely, handprints represent the intentional acts that can offset or even overcome a footprint. They are the compassionate gestures, the inclusive decisions, and the empathetic actions that leave behind positive impressions. Handprints are the catalysts for progress, the bridges between diverse perspectives, and the tools for repairing the world we inhabit.

This book, a unique fusion of music and leadership insights, will guide you on your inclusive leadership journey. Each chapter pairs a thoughtfully chosen song with an inclusive leadership tip, weaving together melody and wisdom. Immerse yourself in the music, let the lyrics resonate with you, and embrace the emotions they stir. As you revisit these songs, they'll help forge a mental soundtrack that enhances your development as an inclusive leader in all aspects of life. Let the power of music lead the way.

ACKNOWLEDGMENTS

To my soulmate, **Dr Chuck Herring**. Thank you for filling our home with music which has been the backdrop to our joys, sorrows, and everything in between. Your unwavering support has allowed our family to create our own mental playlist, a soundtrack that accompanies us on our unique life journeys.

To our three beautiful and talented daughters, **Vanessa**, **Ashley**, and **Imani**, may your mental playlist continue to guide you through the melodies of life with grace and resilience.

I would like to express my heartfelt gratitude to the following individuals, whose contributions have been invaluable in bringing this book to life:

Carol Bobolts with Red Herring Design: Your remarkable book designing talents have given this work a stunning visual identity that captivates readers.

Emily Marko: Your creative illustrations have added a unique dimension to the pages of this book, making it even more engaging.

Marteinn Jonasson with Oddi Sales: Your expertise in book printing has resulted in a magnificently crafted physical copy that we can all be proud of.

Megan O'Brien: Your third party validation and consistent encouragement to get the content done.

Emmai Alaquiva: Your captivating photography brought the cover to life, infusing it with warmth and depth.

Renaé Powell: Your meticulous attention to detail and exceptional proofreading skills have ensured that this book is polished and error-free.

Your dedication and expertise have transformed my vision into reality, and I am truly grateful for your contributions to this project.

PLAYLIST

LEAN ON ME

TRACK
1

45 RPM

BILL WITHERS

Trading Egos for Insights

BE OPEN TO LEARNING FROM OTHERS

There are few songs that have the power to move us, to bring us together, and to inspire us to be better people. "Lean On Me" by Bill Withers is one of those songs.

The lyrics of "Lean On Me" are simple yet profound. They remind us that no matter who we are, we all face challenges and hardships in life. The song speaks to the universality of human experience and encourages us to be understanding and *empathetic* toward others. The lyrics remind us that:

No matter how difficult things may seem, there is always a way forward.

At its core, "Lean On Me" is a song about connection. It emphasizes the importance of building strong relationships with those around us, of reaching out to others in times of need, and of being willing to lend a helping hand. We are reminded throughout the song that we are all in this together, and that we have the power to make a positive impact on the world around us.

One of the most powerful aspects of "Lean On Me" is its message of inclusivity. Regardless of age, race, ability, gender identity, sexual orientation, or any other identifying characteristic, "Lean On Me" encourages us to be open to others and to learn from their experiences. It reminds us that there is always something to learn from the people around us and that diversity and differences should be celebrated, not feared.

In today's world, where divisions and polarization seem to be increasingly common, the message of "Lean On Me" is more important than ever. The song serves as a powerful reminder of the positive impact that can result from supporting one another. It encourages us to be better people, to be more understanding and empathetic toward others, and to build stronger connections with those around us.

"Lean On Me" by Bill Withers is a song that has stood the test of time. Its message of compassion, unity, and connection is as relevant today as it was when it was first released. As you navigate the challenges of being an inclusive leader, remember the lessons contained in this powerful song and add it to your mental playlist.

MENTAL SOUNDTRACK REMIX
Listen to "Lean on Me" and commit to one actionable step towards embracing lessons from those around you.

ENCOURAGE OPEN DIALOGUE & FEEDBACK

As human beings, our natural inclination is to connect and communicate with one another. Expressing ourselves openly and honestly can be a challenge, particularly when giving and receiving feedback. Matt Simons' song "Open Up" suggests that communication can sometimes be challenging. However:

Inclusive leaders excel in dismantling barriers that hinder impactful communication, fostering a more open exchange of ideas.

Building trust is the first step toward encouraging open dialogue. The "wall" that Matt Simons mentions in his song represents the barriers that can exist between leaders and their teams. These barriers can be physical, emotional, or even hierarchical. Inclusive leaders make a conscious effort to break down these walls by fostering an environment of trust, respect, and empathy.

Inclusive leaders listen with curiosity and value diverse perspectives, effectively bridging communication gaps.

Recognizing communication as a two-way street, inclusive leaders proactively bridge gaps with their teams. Not waiting for others to initiate communication, they seek out chances to connect and engage, playing a key role in promoting open dialogue and feedback.

These leaders understand that diversity in thoughts and experiences enriches the team's overall perspective, leading to more innovative and effective solutions. They foster a culture of trust and respect, where differing opinions are actively sought and celebrated. Inclusive leadership means recognizing the unique contributions of each team member and providing them with the tools and opportunities to succeed. Ultimately, their leadership style cultivates a collaborative and empowering atmosphere, where everyone is motivated to contribute their best work. So, let's take a cue from the lyrics of "Open Up" and strive to be inclusive leaders who break down walls, bridge gaps, and encourage open dialogue and feedback to create environments where all team members feel seen, heard, and valued.

MENTAL SOUNDTRACK REMIX
Play "Open Up" and identify one actionable step you will take to foster impactful communication.

INVEST IN YOUR TEAM

John Lennon's "Imagine," an anthem for unity and hope, resonates beyond its call for global peace, extending to inclusive leadership in the workplace. Let's explore how the lyrics of "Imagine" align with the principles of inclusive leadership, and why nurturing and supporting your team is the key to unlocking their full potential.

Inclusive leaders work hard to remove barriers that hinder successful outcomes.

In the opening verse, Lennon invites us to imagine a world without divisions or exclusions. In a similar spirit, inclusive leaders embody this principle in their organizations. They understand the importance of avoiding any form of elitism within their teams. Their focus is on fostering a culture of equity, where every individual is valued and treated with dignity and respect, regardless of their background, gender, race, or other traits.

What does peace look like in the workplace?

Peace in the workplace doesn't mean the absence of conflict but rather a culture of respect, empathy, and understanding. Inclusive leaders foster an atmosphere of harmony by actively addressing conflicts and promoting open communication. They invest in team-building activities, conflict resolution training, and diversity and inclusion initiatives.

Inclusive leaders understand that to bring about change, they need to inspire and motivate their team members to share their vision.

Just as Lennon believed that he was not the only one who imagined a world of peace, inclusive leaders encourage their teams to embrace diversity and foster inclusion, making it a collective effort. Inclusive leadership doesn't stop at the team level. It ripples out into the broader world of business and society. When leaders invest in their teams, they set an example for others to follow. Their inclusive approach can inspire other leaders and organizations to create diverse and inclusive workplaces.

In this way, the world of work can be a more united and harmonious place.

"Imagine" is a powerful reminder of the possibilities that lie within our reach when we dare to dream of a more inclusive world. So, let's heed Lennon's call and *IMAGINE* a world where leaders invest in their teams, making the dream of a more inclusive future a reality.

MENTAL SOUNDTRACK REMIX

Get inspired by "Imagine" and identify one step you will take to strengthen your team.

REACH

TRACK 4

45 RPM

The Clarity Chronicles

GLORIA ESTEFAN

DREAMS

ESTABLISH CLEAR EXPECTATIONS & GOALS

In the dynamic realm of leadership, setting clear expectations and goals is the compass that guides a team toward success. Gloria Estefan's song "Reach" echoes this, reminding us that dreams need direction and commitment to become reality.

Dreams are the seeds of our goals, nurturing them with passion and perseverance leads to the blossoming of achievements.

At its core, "Reach" is a song about overcoming obstacles and reaching for your dreams. The lyrics encourage listeners to never give up, even when the path ahead seems difficult or uncertain. But in order to reach those dreams, you need to have a clear understanding of what you're working toward. That's where setting clear expectations and goals comes in.

On your inclusive leadership journey, setting clear expectations and goals is essential for motivating and inspiring teams. When individuals know exactly what is expected of them and what they're working toward, they're more likely to feel motivated and engaged in their work. They're also better equipped to prioritize their tasks and make decisions that align with the organization's goals.

But setting clear expectations isn't just about motivating people. It's also a crucial element of

MENTAL SOUNDTRACK REMIX
Let "Reach" inspire you to reflect on steps you can take to establish clear expectations and goals.

impactful communication. When expectations are unclear or constantly changing, people can become confused or frustrated. This can lead to a breakdown in communication, which can have negative consequences for the organization as a whole.

Setting clear expectations and goals is essential, as it charts a defined path to REACH your dreams with focus and determination.

In the world of leadership, setting clear expectations and goals is akin to setting the stage for success. Inclusive leaders who understand the value of diversity and actively work to create an inclusive environment, have a unique responsibility to ensure that their teams are aligned, motivated, and empowered to achieve greatness. This is the essence of inclusive leadership—bringing people together, setting a clear course, and nurturing the collective dream until it becomes a timeless reality.

RECOGNIZE AND EMBRACE DIVERSITY

Music's ability to inspire and empower transcends borders, cultures and languages. "Brown Girl" by Aaradhna is a prime example, offering an uplifting message to women of color.

Be proud of who you are,
don't let society's expectations
or stereotypes hold you back.

Aaradhna speaks to the struggles that many women of color face in a world that often values Eurocentric beauty standards. Aaradhna reminds listeners that their worth and beauty are not defined by societal norms or the opinions of others. Instead, they should be proud of their unique backgrounds, cultures, and experiences.

Aaradhna also highlights the importance of representation and visibility. The song urges young women of color to take up space, to be heard, and to be seen.

You are not invisible.
Your voice matters.
You are more than enough.

This message is incredibly powerful and relevant not only to young women of color but to anyone who has ever felt marginalized or excluded. Each member of your team has something valuable to contribute, and by recognizing and embracing diversity, you can unlock the full potential of your team. And, let them know:

They are not invisible.
Their voice matters.
They are more than enough.

Remind them that their unique perspectives enrich the collective understanding and drive innovation. Encourage them to share their ideas and experiences, as these are the keys to growth and success. Reassure them that their efforts are valued and acknowledge their achievements. Embrace the opportunity to create a welcoming space where all individuals prosper and experience a deep sense of community.

MENTAL SOUNDTRACK REMIX
Crank up "Brown Girl" and let its powerful message move you to acknowledge and celebrate diversity.

TRACK

6

45
RPM

Failosophy

**WE ARE THE
CHAMPIONS**
QUEEN

LEARN FROM FAILURE

Queen's "We Are The Champions" is a song that not only celebrates victory and success but also highlights the hard work, perseverance, and inevitable failures along the way. The ability to learn from our failures and use them as stepping stones toward greatness is what sets true champions apart from the rest.

The opening line of the song highlights the hard work and sacrifice that is required to reach the top. Often, failure is seen as a setback, a sign that we are not good enough or that our efforts have been in vain. But the reality is that failure is an essential part of the learning process. You must make mistakes and fail in order to learn and grow.

The basketball odyssey of Lebron James stands as a prime example of how failure can serve as a powerful catalyst for growth. As one of the greatest players of all time, James has achieved remarkable success in his career, largely due to using defeat as a tool for advancement.

Despite facing multiple setbacks, including several losses in the NBA Finals, James never surrendered to despair. Rather than succumbing to defeat or wallowing in disappointment, he consistently employed these experiences to invigorate himself and elevate his team members. The following speaks to James' resolve:

Persist in your struggle because there's no room for defeat, for every step you take is a victory in itself.

After a crushing loss in the 2011 NBA Finals, James famously declared that he would not let it define him and vowed to emerge as a better player. He fulfilled that promise, capturing four NBA championships and earning four NBA Finals MVP awards in the years since.

"We Are The Champions" by Queen is not just a song about winning. It is a song about the journey toward success and the role that failure plays in that journey. Failure is not the opposite of success; it is an essential part of it. Inclusive leaders embrace failure, learn from it, and use it as a stepping stone toward greater success. Let us remember that inclusive leaders are:

True champions who learn from their failures and come back even stronger.

MENTAL SOUNDTRACK REMIX
Listen to "We Are The Champions" and let it fuel your determination to embrace a champion's mindset.

ON YOUR FACE

TRACK 7

45 RPM

EARTH, WIND & FIRE

Facial Diplomacy

TEACH YOUR FACIAL EXPRESSIONS TO USE THEIR INSIDE VOICES

**Inclusive leadership is about creating a culture of belonging, respect, and equity.
It involves impactful communication, both verbal and non-verbal.
Your facial expressions are a powerful form of non-verbal communication,
and they can either build bridges or erect barriers within your team.**

Earth, Wind & Fire's classic hit, "On Your Face," is a powerful example of the connection between facial expressions and emotions.

Our emotions are often reflected on our face, revealing our true feelings.
Even when we attempt to mask them, they reveal our story.

In your role as an inclusive leader, being mindful of the messages you're sending with your facial expressions is essential. For example, if you are in a meeting and you're frowning or scowling, your team members may interpret that as disapproval or anger, even if you're just deep in thought. Alternatively, if you're smiling and nodding, your team members may feel more comfortable and confident, even if you're not saying anything at all.

Being aware of your facial expressions is especially important when it comes to creating an inclusive workplace. People from different cultures may interpret facial expressions differently. For example, in some cultures, direct eye contact is seen as a sign of respect and engagement, while in others, it may be seen as aggressive or disrespectful.

It is important to recognize and adapt to diverse communication styles while being mindful of your own biases and how they may be influencing your

MENTAL SOUNDTRACK REMIX

Get energized by "On Your Face" to make sure your facial expressions truly reflect your inner voice.

facial expressions. For instance, if you have a negative bias toward a particular group of people, you may unconsciously express that bias through your facial expressions.

Inclusive leadership is all about creating a workplace where EVERYONE feels valued and respected, regardless of their lived experiences or identity. Paying attention to your facial expressions is just one small but important step toward achieving that goal. So let's make sure that what's "On Your Face" is inclusive, respectful, and welcoming to all. In other words, ***Teach Your Facial Expressions To Use Their Inside Voices***.

TRACK

8

45
RPM

EVERY BREATH
YOU TAKE
THE POLICE

A Thin Line Between Love and Hate

ARE YOU MACRO LEADING OR MICROMANAGING?

Impactful leadership is like conducting a symphony: the leader sets the pace, fosters harmony, and directs, trusting and empowering their team to apply their expertise. This approach promotes a harmonious and efficient work environment.

On the other hand, the lyrics from "Every Breath You Take" by The Police, convey an:

Overbearing and relentless form of supervision, often characterized by micromanagement.

Such a hands-on approach can suppress creativity, decrease productivity, and diminish team trust. Overseeing every tiny detail creates a stifling atmosphere.

Conversely, ***macro leadership*** highlights and nurtures the unique strengths and creativity within your team, fostering an environment where they can flourish. Picture an inclusive leader as an orchestra conductor, who skillfully inspires and guides the ensemble without playing each instrument. This approach fosters collaboration and steers the team toward collective achievements, cultivating a harmonious and effective workplace.

Drawing inspiration from "Every Breath You Take," inclusive leadership is about overseeing your team not to dominate, but to support and guide them. While inclusive leaders may need to monitor certain processes, it's crucial to avoid stifling individual creativity. People yearn for guidance, not control.

In the art of leadership, it's essential to reflect and ask yourself: "Am I macro leading or micromanaging?" True inclusive leadership zooms out to the bigger picture, cultivating trust and open communication while stepping away from rigid control. This style nurtures a supportive atmosphere, boosting team confidence and ownership, which ultimately leads to heightened morale and productivity.

MENTAL SOUNDTRACK REMIX
Put on "Every Breath You Take" and be inspired toward Macro Leadership, steering clear of the pitfalls of Micromanaging.

PROVIDE TEAM MEMBERS WITH LEADERSHIP OPPORTUNITIES

How often do we consider the hidden leadership potential within our teams? Success in any organization relies on leaders at all levels, not just at the top. Encouraging team members to take on leadership roles fosters personal growth, and drives collaboration and innovation throughout the organization.

Andra Day's uplifting anthem, "Rise Up," serves not only as a call to action but also as a poignant reminder of the resilience and potential inherent in each of us. Cultivating leadership within your team transcends mere necessity; it is a transformative strategy. But the question remains: how can you foster a culture that encourages team members to step forward and lead?

Setting the Stage for Emerging Leaders
The first step to nurturing leadership is acknowledging each team member's unique strengths. Leadership transcends the notion of a single person. It, instead, thrives on opportunities where everyone has the chance to lead in their own way. Additionally, it fosters an environment that encourages initiative and views failures as valuable lessons which paves the way for greater understanding and expertise.

Offering leadership opportunities means providing challenges that stimulate growth. These can be leading projects, spearheading cross-departmental initiatives, or conducting training sessions. Each opportunity stretches team members' capabilities, aligning with the spirit of "Rise Up," which speaks to finding the strength to overcome adversity with grace and courage.

Building Resilience
Leadership is as much about resilience as it is about guiding others. Embed the principles of resilience by encouraging persistence, teaching stress management techniques, and showing how to gracefully handle setbacks. Just as Andra Day's song emphasizes perseverance, encourage your team members to see each challenge as an opportunity to learn and grow.

Empowerment
Empowering your team to lead is akin to a chorus in a song—each voice strengthens the melody. As the voices "Rise Up," so does the collective capability of your team. Let the spirit of Andra Day's anthem remind us that with the right support and opportunities, everyone has the potential to lead.

MENTAL SOUNDTRACK REMIX
Embrace the empowering message of "Rise Up" and uplift and create growth opportunities for your team members.

OFFER FLEXIBILITY IN WORK ARRANGEMENTS

The landscape of the world of work has undergone a remarkable transformation influenced by new technologies and evolving work cultures.

At the forefront of this transformation are inclusive leaders who recognize the value of flexibility and are willing to provide it to their team members. They understand that every person is different and has diverse needs and preferences, and that a one-size-fits-all approach to work arrangements is no longer viable. Inclusive leaders provide their team members with the support and resources they need to overcome personal challenges and achieve professional success, resulting in a happier and more productive workforce.

Faith Evans' song "Change," beautifully captures the sentiment that:

As a collective, we possess the power
To initiate transformative change in our lives.
And, if we sow the seeds of support,
A brighter path toward success can be paved.

The verse that alludes to sowing seeds and extending a helping hand serves as a poignant reminder that inclusive leaders willingly go above and beyond. They shoulder the responsibility of ensuring that everyone is afforded equitable opportunities for success.

A flexible work arrangement is more than just an organizational perk. It represents a commitment to recognizing that each of us is guided by a personal destiny. By enabling employees to find a work-life balance that suits their individual needs, leaders are essentially allowing them to shape their destinies. This not only benefits the individual but also propels the organization forward with motivated, fulfilled, and dedicated team members.

For example, remote work and flexible hours enable employees to seamlessly balance their professional responsibilities with personal commitments, enhancing productivity and reducing stress. Additionally, job sharing further eases this balance by allowing two employees to split a full-time role, lightening the workload and creating more time for other pursuits.

While implementing these types of arrangements comes with its own set of challenges, the rewards of working together to overcome these obstacles can be significant. As reflected in the song, when we lead the charge for change and extend our support, we lay the foundation for a work environment that is not only inclusive but also fosters productivity and harmony.

MENTAL SOUNDTRACK REMIX

Play "Change" and lead the charge for change in work arrangements.

MULTIPLY THE STRENGTHS AROUND YOU

Achieving success often relies on more than just individual effort and strengths. Recognizing the power of collaboration and utilizing the strengths of others is essential.

This idea is exquisitely encapsulated in the song "Make Me Better" by Fabolous featuring Ne-Yo. In the song, Fabolous reminds us that:

Together, we are stronger

The lyrics of this song emphasize the importance of combining strengths to achieve greater results. When we work together, we can achieve more than we ever could alone.

One way to multiply the strengths around you is to create a diverse team. Rather than surrounding yourself with people who think and act just like you, seek out individuals who bring different perspectives and strengths to the table. This could mean hiring employees with different skill sets or seeking out mentors with unique experiences.

The African proverb, "If you want to go fast, go alone. If you want to go far, go together," emphasizes the importance of collaboration and teamwork. This saying highlights the fact that we can achieve our goals faster when we work alone, but we can go further when we work together.

However, going together doesn't guarantee success if there isn't trust in the relationship. Trust is a vital component of any successful collaboration, and it is necessary for any group to function effectively. Trust allows people to rely on each other, to communicate openly, and to work together toward a common goal.

The concept of trust and collaboration resonates deeply in "Make Me Better." Its lyrics emphasize that:

On our own we can make an impact but when we unite, we become an unstoppable force.

The lyrics speak to the idea that we can be more than just our individual strengths and weaknesses; together we can be a collective force that is greater than the sum of its parts. A true testament to the incredible synergy that collaboration can unleash.

MENTAL SOUNDTRACK REMIX
Listen to "Make Me Better" and reflect on how you will use the strengths of those around you to amplify collective achievement.

NEITHER ONE
OF US (WANTS TO BE
THE FIRST TO SAY GOODBYE)

TRACK
12

45
RPM

The Altruist's Dilemma

GLADYS KNIGHT
& THE PIPS

EXIT

MAKE TOUGH DECISIONS FOR THE GREATER GOOD

Gladys Knight & The Pips' ballad "Neither One Of Us" mirrors the tough decision of parting ways, similar to an inclusive leader's dilemma of letting someone go for the benefit of the team. To navigate these decisions while maintaining inclusivity, the 4A Framework–Awareness, Action, Assess, and Again–offers essential guidance.

Awareness

Inclusive leaders can detect potential issues by employing proactive measures like ongoing performance evaluations and regular check-ins. Early identification of struggles allows leaders the opportunity to intervene and offer support.

Action

Before making any difficult decisions, ensure that the team member has received ample support and opportunities for growth. This can include mentoring, coaching, or access to workshops. By doing so, leaders demonstrate their commitment to inclusivity and professional growth.

The overall well-being and success of the entire team must be considered. If a team member's performance or behavior negatively impacts others, weigh the potential benefits of retaining the individual versus the harm being done to the team's morale, productivity, and cohesion. If letting a team member go is deemed necessary, approach the situation with empathy, honesty, and transparency.

Assess & Again

Inclusive leaders continuously learn and grow from these challenging experiences. They reflect on the situation, identify areas for improvement, and apply those learnings to future situations. Inclusive leadership is a delicate integration of nurturing growth, promoting inclusive principles, and making tough decisions for the greater good of the team. The goal is not to avoid making hard decisions, but rather to approach them thoughtfully and responsibly, always keeping inclusivity at the forefront. As the song reminds us, saying goodbye is never easy, but with intentionality and empathy, inclusive leaders can navigate these difficult decisions while maintaining a supportive and collaborative environment.

MENTAL SOUNDTRACK REMIX

Play "Neither One Of Us (Wants To Be The First To Say Goodbye)" and reflect on leveraging the 4A Framework when faced with making tough decisions.

CELEBRATE SUCCESS

Kool & The Gang's famous song, "Celebration" reminds us to pause and celebrate all wins, big or small; each is a step toward success. Recognizing these moments uplifts the team and builds a culture of appreciation and achievement.

An impromptu dance party is a fantastic and fun way to celebrate big and small wins.

Let's explore other ways to create a culture of appreciation by actively celebrating the contributions and successes of your team.

Acknowledge the Unsung Heroes

In any team, there are often individuals who silently go above and beyond to ensure tasks are completed successfully. As an inclusive leader, it's crucial to recognize and appreciate their unwavering dedication. Take the time to highlight their contributions, whether it's through public recognition during team meetings, a heartfelt email, or even a simple shout-out on a company communication platform. By acknowledging the unsung heroes, you not only make them feel valued but also inspire others to go the extra mile.

Cultivate a Culture of Appreciation

Celebrating success shouldn't be a one-time event; it should be ingrained in the fabric of your organization's culture. Encourage team members to recognize and appreciate one another's efforts regularly. Foster an environment where individuals feel comfortable expressing gratitude, be it through peer-to-peer recognition programs, feedback sessions, or team-building activities that promote camaraderie. By making appreciation a core value, you create a positive and motivating workplace where everyone feels seen and valued.

Share the Spotlight

Success is achieved through collective effort. When your team reaches a milestone or completes a challenging project, celebrate together to acknowledge achievements and foster unity. Organize a team outing or special event to show gratitude. Playing Kool & The Gang's "Celebration" during gatherings can uplift spirits and remind everyone of their collective hard work and success.

MENTAL SOUNDTRACK REMIX
Turn up "Celebration" and have a dance party while you reflect on ways to acknowledge your team's large and small wins.

OUTRO

As we conclude Volume 1 of our exploration of inclusive leadership and embark on the final chapter of our journey, it is crucial to take a moment for reflection. Throughout this voyage, we have delved into the profound lessons that inclusive leadership imparts. Each day, we are presented with a fundamental choice: to either unknowingly contribute harm or consciously engage in the healing, uplifting, and betterment of our world. As we stand at this juncture, let us remember that our guiding beacon has been music—a universal language that resonates with our emotions and ignites our spirits. These melodies will continue to serve as a wellspring of strength and wisdom on your enduring journey of self-awareness and transformation.

While the final notes softly serenade us in the background, it is vital to recognize that our journey does not reach its conclusion here. The power to create a more compassionate world resides within each of us, so:

Embrace the 4 A Framework—Awareness, Action, Assess, and Again.

Be mindful of both your footprints—the negative marks you leave behind in your wake—and your handprints—the positive impacts you consciously make. Remember "handprints heal footprints!"

Your journey toward self-awareness and transformation is not finite; rather, it is a lifelong endeavor. With each step, you are presented with an opportunity to contribute to a world that is more empathetic and inclusive.

I hope that Mind Jukebox inspires you to remix your mental soundtracks often. Remember, each tune we adjust and each note we refine can lead to profound shifts in our mental and emotional landscapes. Let's continue to embrace the power of change. Thank you for being an essential part of this adventure. Stay tuned for the release of Volume 2, where we'll continue to explore the mental playlists that shape our lives.

ABOUT THE AUTHOR

Dr. Christine Herring is an educator and a lifelong learner at heart. Her passion for teaching extends beyond the classroom, touching the lives of those around her. Married to her best friend, she cherishes the joy of family life, finding happiness in the bustling energy of her loved ones. Christine's enthusiasm for continuous learning keeps her ever-curious and engaged with the world. Driven by a desire to inspire and uplift, she dedicates herself to helping others become the best versions of themselves. Her warm, nurturing spirit and commitment to education and personal growth are the pillars that define her both professionally and personally.

LINER NOTES

"Lean on Me"
ARTIST: Bill Withers
ALBUM: *Still Bill*
RELEASE DATE: 1972
LABEL: Sussex Records
SONGWRITER: Bill Withers

"Open Up"
ARTIST: Matt Simons
ALBUM: *After the Landslide*
RELEASE DATE: 2019
LABEL: Matt Simons Music
SONGWRITERS: Matt Simons,
Lars De Wee, and Jamie Hartman

"Imagine"
ARTIST: John Lennon
ALBUM: *Imagine*
RELEASE DATE: 1971
LABEL: Apple Records
Songwriters: John Lennon

"Reach"
ARTIST: Gloria Estefan
ALBUM: *Destiny*
RELEASE DATE: 1996
LABEL: Epic Records
SONGWRITERS: Gloria Estefan,
Diane Warren

"Brown Girl"
ARTIST: Aaradhna
ALBUM: *Brown Girl*
RELEASE DATE: 2016
LABEL: Frequency Media Group
SONGWRITERS: Aaradhna Patel,
Jeff Dynamite

"We Are The Champions"
ARTIST: Queen
ALBUM: *News of the World*
RELEASE DATE: 1977
LABEL: EMI Records,
Elektra Records
SONGWRITER: Freddie Mercury

"On Your Face"
ARTIST: Earth, Wind & Fire
ALBUM: *Spirit*
RELEASE DATE: 1976
LABEL: Columbia Records
SONGWRITERS: Maurice White,
Charles Stepney, Philip Bailey

"Every Breath You Take"
ARTIST: The Police
ALBUM: *Synchronicity*
RELEASE DATE: 1983
LABEL: A&M Records
SONGWRITER: Sting

"Rise Up"
ARTIST: Andra Day
ALBUM: *Cheers to the Fall*
RELEASE DATE: 2015
LABEL: Warner Bros. Records
SONGWRITERS: Cassandra Batie,
Jennifer Decilveo

"Change"
ARTIST: Faith Evans
ALBUM: "Keep the Faith"
RELEASE DATE: 1998
LABEL: Bad Boy Records
SONGWRITERS: Faith Evans,
Sean Combs, Ron Lawrence

"Make Me Better"
ARTIST: Fabolous *featuring*
Ne-Yo
ALBUM: *From Nothin' to Somethin'*
RELEASE DATE: 2007
LABEL: Def Jam Recordings
SONGWRITERS: John Jackson,
Shaffer Smith, Eric Hudson,
Timothy Mosley

**"Neither One of Us (Wants to
Be the First to Say Goodbye)"**
ARTIST: Gladys Knight & the Pips
ALBUM: *Neither One of Us*
RELEASE DATE: 1973
LABEL: Motown Records
SONGWRITER: Jim Weatherly

"Celebration"
ARTIST: Kool & the Gang
ALBUM: *Celebrate!*
RELEASE DATE: 1980
LABEL: De-Lite Records
SONGWRITERS: Ronald Bell,
Claydes Charles Smith, George
Brown, J.T. Taylor, Robert Spike
Mickens, Earl Toon Jr., Dennis
Thomas, Robert Bell